This Is What I Want to Be

Teacher

Heather Miller

Heinemann Library
Chicago, Illinois

©2003 Reed Educational & Professional Publishing
Published by Heinemann Library,
an imprint of Reed Educational & Professional Publishing
Chicago, IL

Customer Service 888-454-2279
Visit our website at www.heinemannlibrary.com

Designed by Sue Emerson, Heinemann Library
Printed and bound in the United States by Lake Book Manufacturing, Inc.

07 06 05 04
10 9 8 7 6 5 4 3

Library of Congress Cataloging-in-Publication Data
Miller, Heather.
    Teacher / Heather Miller.
      p. cm. — (This is what I want to be)
Includes index.
Summary: A simple introduction to the equipment, uniform, daily duties,
and other aspects of the job of a police officer.
    ISBN: 1-4034-0372-4 (HC), 1-4034-0594-8 (Pbk.)
    1. Teachers—Juvenile literature. 2. Teaching—Vocational guidance—Juvenile literature.
[1. Teachers. 2. Teaching. 3. Occupations.] I. Title.
LB1775 .M613 2002
371.1—dc21

2001008139

Acknowledgments
The author and publishers are grateful to the following for permission to reproduce copyright material:
pp. 4, 6, 11, 15, 18 Brian Warling/Heinemann Library; p. 5 Ernest Braun/Stone/Getty Images; p. 7 Steve Benbow/Stock Boston; pp. 8, 9R Gary Rhijnsburger/Masterfile; p. 9L David Young-Wolfe/PhotoEdit; p. 10 Charles Shoffner/Index Stock Imagery, Inc.; p. 12 Clark Weinberg/The Image Bank/Getty Images; p. 13 Jim Pickerell/Alamy/Stock Connection, Inc.; p. 14 Jay Thomas/International Stock; pp. 16, 17L Lawrence Migdale; p. 17R Doug Menuez/Stock Boston; p. 19 Cheryl A. Ertelt/Visuals Unlimited; p. 20 Pictor International, Ltd./PictureQuest; p. 21 Richard Nowitz/Photo Researchers, Inc.; p. 23 (row 1, L-R) Joe Atlas/Brand X Pictures, David Young-Wolfe/PhotoEdit; p.23 (row 2, L-R) Joe Atlas/Brand X Pictures, Eric Fowke/PhotoEdit; (row 3) Brian Warling/Heinemann Library

Cover photograph by Masterfile
Photo research by Scott Braut

Special thanks to our advisory panel for their help in the preparation of this book:

Eileen Day, Preschool Teacher
Chicago, IL

Ellen Dolmetsch, MLS
Wilmington, DE

Kathleen Gilbert,
Second Grade Teacher
Austin, TX

Sandra Gilbert,
Library Media Specialist
Houston, TX

Angela Leeper,
Educational Consultant
North Carolina Department
of Public Instruction
Raleigh, NC

Pam McDonald, Reading Teacher
Winter Springs, FL

Melinda Murphy,
Library Media Specialist
Houston, TX

Special thanks to the faculty and students of Stockton School, Chicago, IL, for their help in the preparation of this book.

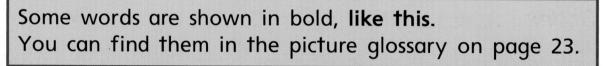
Some words are shown in bold, **like this.**
You can find them in the picture glossary on page 23.

Contents

What Do Teachers Do?

Teachers help people learn.

They read stories and answer questions.

Teachers like to make learning fun.

They plan special projects and trips.

What Is a Teacher's Day Like?

Teachers' days are very busy.

They get the **classroom** ready every morning.

Teachers help every child in the class.

They give tests and listen to children read.

What Tools Do Teachers Use?

Teachers use **chalk**.

They write on a **chalkboard**.

Teachers use **computers.**

They use pens and paper, too.

Where Do Teachers Work?

Teachers work in schools.

There are many teachers in each school.

Most teachers have their own **classroom.**

Do Teachers Work in Other Places?

Teachers can work in **hospitals.**

They teach children who are sick.

Some teachers work at home.

They teach their own children.

When Do Teachers Work?

Teachers work every day except Saturday and Sunday.

Most teachers work in the daytime.

Teachers stay at school after students go home.

They get ready for the next day.

What Special Things Do Teachers Do?

Some teachers help children with special needs.

They teach children who cannot hear or see.

Some teachers help children learn to speak better.

Other teachers teach children who speak different languages.

What Kinds of Teachers Are There?

Substitute teachers do not teach every day.

They teach when other teachers get sick.

Some teachers teach only art or music.

This teacher is teaching gym class.

How Do People Become Teachers?

People go to college to learn to become teachers.

They learn from other teachers, too.

Teachers must practice teaching.

Teachers are people who love
to learn.

Quiz

Can you remember what these things are called?

Look for the answers on page 24.

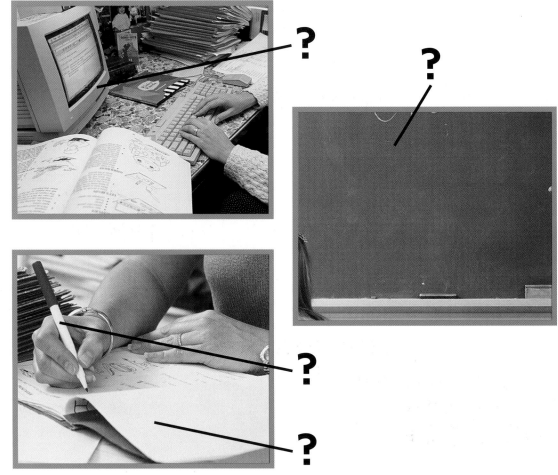

Picture Glossary

chalk
page 8

computer
page 9

chalkboard
page 8

hospital
page 12

classroom
pages 6, 11

Note to Parents and Teachers

Reading for information is an important part of a child's literacy development. Learning begins with a question about something. Help children think of themselves as investigators and researchers by encouraging their questions about the world around them. Each chapter in this book begins with a question. Read the question together. Look at the pictures. Talk about what you think the answer might be. Then read the text to find out if your predictions were correct. Think of other questions you could ask about the topic, and discuss where you might find the answers. Assist children in using the picture glossary and the index to practice new vocabulary and research skills.

Index

Answers to quiz on page 22

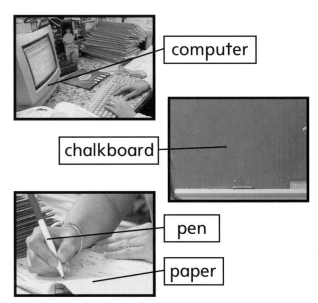

computer

chalkboard

pen

paper